STARKEY'S BOOK OF STATES

Other Books by David Starkey

Starkey's Book of States
(ebook version)

STARKEY'S BOOK OF STATES

Poetry
by
David Starkey

Drawings
by
Rafael Perea de la Cabada

BOSON BOOKS
Raleigh

BOSON

Published by
Boson Books, a division of C & M Online Media, Inc.
3905 Meadow Field Lane,
Raleigh, NC 27606-4470
cm@cmonline.com

http://www.bosonbooks.com

ISBN (paper): 1-932482-54-7
ISBN (ebook): 1-886420-21-1

All drawings are from the Drawing Room series and are copyrighted
by Rafael Perea de la Cabada.

Dedication

To our wives, Sandy and Ronda

Table of Contents

Preface

As a child, I was fascinated by maps. I'd pore over them, losing myself on the highways and in the river valleys, traveling to cities and towns far, far away from my tract house in Sacramento, California. An atlas was a portal to another world.

Not surprisingly, when I began writing poetry in my early twenties, readers often remarked on the strong sense of place the poems evoked. I'd frequently turn to maps for inspiration, and as I began publishing my work, it struck me that it would be a worthwhile endeavor to publish a poem in at least one literary journal in every state of the Union. Now *that* would be an American adventure. At Francis Marion University in Florence, South Carolina, where I taught for the first half of the 1990s, my colleagues would ask me—facetiously, yes, but also, I thought, with a hint of grudging respect—whether or not I'd "gotten any new states." Often I could answer in the affirmative, though Delaware was proving to be a bit of problem.

In the midst of my quest, I came upon a tattered children's geography primer in a second-hand store, *The Arrow Book of States*, and I soon became absorbed with the idea of writing a poem *set* in every state. Perhaps I was suffering from an undiagnosed case of *topomania*: the poetic map I was making was a bit crazy, an idiosyncratic assortment of people, places and events. It ranged across time and space, stealing into the minds of anonymous working people, but also looking at famous Americans like Emerson and John Brown, Sojourner Truth and Phillis Wheatley.

In 1995, when Nancy and David McAllister offered to publish *Starkey's Book of States* as an e-book, I gladly accepted their offer. I didn't know anything about online publishing, but it sounded fun, and, who knew what possibilities such a format might offer? Maybe I'd become the Walt Whitman of the Internet.

That didn't happen, alas, and for more than a decade this collection of poetry basically remained in electronic storage. I moved onto other poems, other projects. I left South Carolina for Illinois, and finally headed back to California.

Then in the summer of 2005 I was surfing the Boson Books Website, and I noticed that there were significantly more print titles than when I'd first sent David and Nancy my manuscript. The nature of publishing had been transformed yet again, with micro-presses and on-demand publishing making it easier—and considerably cheaper—to print books of poetry. I emailed Nancy and asked if she'd be interested in doing a print version of *Starkey's Book of States*, and she happily agreed. Nancy's one recommendation was that I find an artist to illustrate the book.

At first I hesitated. Illustrator Wayne Hogan had made drawings for my book *Open Mike Night at the Cabaret Voltaire* some years before, and while I admired the drawings on their own, in the end they didn't seem to complement the poems against which they were juxtaposed.

Then I thought of my friend and colleague at Santa Barbara City College, Rafael Perea de la Cabada, whose work had lately been receiving international attention. Rafael graciously allowed me to use his work; his only request was that the images be *suggestive* of the poems, not merely *illustrative*. Fortunately, in the course of several pleasant afternoons spent in Rafael's studio looking through boxes of drawings, I found a number of pieces that weren't simply objective correlatives, but seemed, rather, to deepen the poems' mysteries.

Naturally, as the book came closer to print, I considered a wholesale revision: surely I'd learned something about writing poems in the 15 years since some of them had been written. However, as I reread the work, I often found it impossible to reenter a poem's imaginative world, its point of origin. Many of the poems were written in Louisiana and South Carolina, and my first-hand knowledge of the South had faded. Moreover, I discovered that my voice had changed; it had become more genteel—not necessarily a positive development for a poet. These poems are rough around the edges. They often don't begin or end where one would expect. The speakers are frequently hallucinatory, or trying to become that way. Ultimately, I decided to offer up this collection of 52 poems with only the lightest of revisions. *Stet*, as the copyeditors say: *Let it stand.*

What you will find in this book is a word-atlas consisting of an envoi followed by one poem for every state, plus the District of Columbia. This is my *Mappa Americana*, the work of a minor poet obsessed with the country of his birth.

Acknowledgments

Thanks to the editors of the following magazines where some of these poems originally appeared:

Anemone: "Driving North After the Funeral"
Art:Mag: "The Silver City Motel"
The Arts Journal: "North Carolina"
The Beloit Poetry Journal: "Pottawatomie Creek"
Bellowing Ark: "New Frontiers," "True Love Apparent in Idabel, Oklahoma"
Calliope: "Snapshot of My Sister and Brother-in-Law"
Chattahoochee Review: "Antique," "Emerson: Concord, 1882"
Chariton Review: "Miscarriage"
Cumberland Poetry Review: "Rocky Mountain Women's Studies"
Drop Forge: "New Haven Predicament," "Security Parking"
Fine Madness: "Sleeping with Shih Min Lu"
Folio: "Short History of a Woman with a Tattooed Scalp"
Galley Sail Review: "Kin Song in L.A."
Idiom 23 [Australia]: "When I Saw the Swastika"
Imago [Australia]: "Thing"
The Little Magazine: "Phillis Wheatley in East Chicago"
The Lowell Pearl: "Taking the Kids to Washington, DC"
Painted Hills Review: "Illegal Alien"
Piedmont Literary Review: "Bay St. Louis"
Poet Lore: "Portland," "This Poem Is Not About Charleston, South Carolina"
Poetry Motel: "Allen Ginsberg in the Maine Woods"
Santa Fe Sun: "Council Bluffs, 1959"
Slow Dancer [U.K.]: "Dog Eat Dog"
Tampa Bay Review: "Suburban Ghosts"
Whiskey Island Magazine: "Mary Ellen Baker Muses...."
The Widener Review: "Expectant Father: Bad Trip"

Wind: "Watching a Full Moon Rise Above Scapegoat Mountain"
Wisconsin Review: "Plantation Row"

E-Z Off / E-Z On

A welcome sign it is, eight hundred miles
Into a two-day drive. Clenched hands relax,
Your lower back slackens. The stiff trials
Of highway travel melt, like candied wax
Left on the dash, when the right exit comes.
Burger King. Taco Bell. Motel 6. Shell
Station. They line the frontage road like plums
For the picking. Lifting your arm, you smell
The scent of open road. Next morning, fuel
Up, light up, peel out. With what can be carried
In one suitcase, you jet: keen as a boy
In his first car, lover of motion, fool
For life so condensed you might be buried
Alive beneath spadefuls of your own joy.

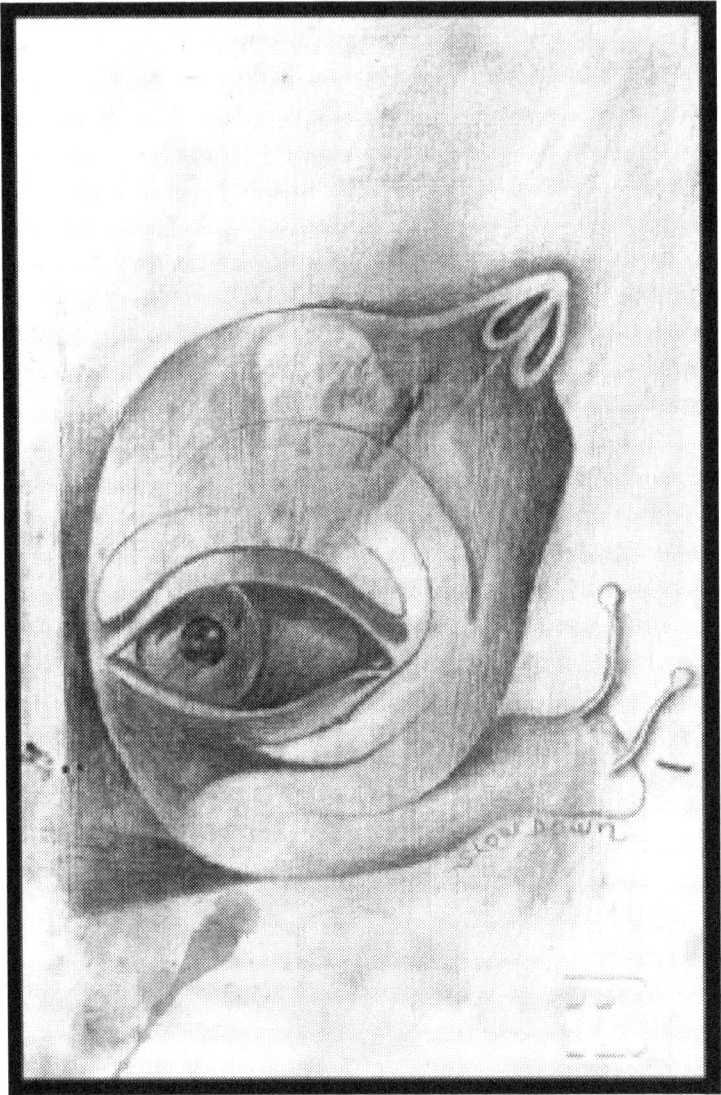

2

SOUTH

The Decline of the Greek Revival in Virginia

They lived before the invention of jazz
But men of power then were prescient

They built great columned houses
In their own version of the classical mode

Massive porticoes, iron grillwork
This was the architecture of fear

Of fortresses besieged
Erected against the times to come

When well-dressed white men would stand alone
In Richmond and Petersburg

Clutching fistfuls of change
On dark street corners

While angry black men circled
Waiting for their chance

The age arrived of fires
Stone and brick façades crumbling

And Dread appeared like a new branch of music
Like Coltrane's *Ascension*

With dim, uncertain precedent
Without climax and resolve

North Carolina

Sampled from The Arrow Book of States, *1961*

Only Texas has more farms than North Carolina.
Only Texas.
        And on this rich land
farmers raise cotton, corn, tobacco, and
peanuts.
       Peanuts.
          North Carolina scientists
have developed an atomic peanut!
They call it NC 4X.
They have developed it.
          An atomic peanut!
Only Texas has more farms than North Carolina,
yet North Carolina has an atomic peanut.
And Texas has none.
There is absolutely no evidence
that Texas
      has
        an
       atomic
         peanut.
These extra-large peanuts are grown from seeds exposed to
atomic radiation. In North Carolina,
land of cotton, corn, tobacco,
        and peanuts.

Driving North After the Funeral

Past the shopping malls of Mobile
Toward the bounty of Birmingham
And beyond, daughters
Squabbling in the backseat:
Their mother guides our traffic like a saint.

Alive in Baton Rouge
She always promised nothing
Less than plenty,
Nothing more than herself,
Hinted each state was a chance

To thresh our needs from wants.
When she died her eyes blossomed
White as dogwoods
And we sold everything,
So that crossing the Escambia

We are a family entirely bound
To time and place.
Even now Mississippi is distant infancy;
Tennessee, an afterlife
We may or may not attain.

Generals of the Confederacy Reborn in a Little Rock Bar

They're all slouched in this grim dive
Smoking Camels, chewing Red Man
Feeding quarters to the dented jukebox
"Who turned on that rock and roll shit?"

How they got here doesn't matter
The South abounds with miracles
Angels cuddle the black night with preachers
Midnight ghosts hum "Cotton Fields"

Look: Tom Jackson's bent low over the eight ball
While Jubal Early taps the floor with his cue
Nathan Forrest cleans his nails with a buck knife
And Old Pete Longstreet keeps missing the spittoon

Tangled beards flecked with gray
Hair half-combed with a smear of grease
Eyes that glare, flinty, unblinking
Watching patiently for one false move

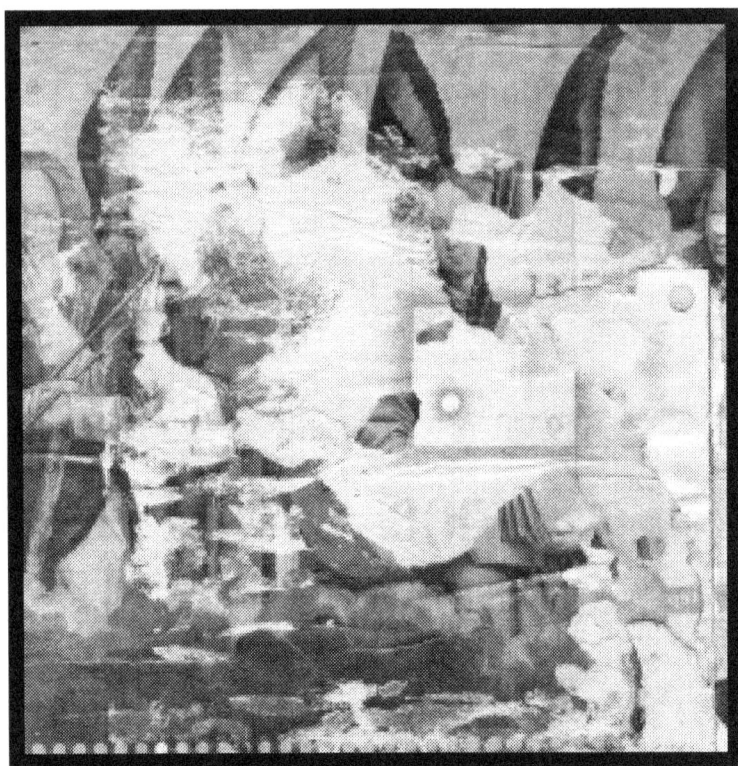

Plantation Row

I stepped out from a doll's house,
1935. Grandfather
built it himself—glazed the windows,
painted pink the miniature chairs.
One foot on the clipped grass

and it sprang up past my ankles.
In the greenhouse
someone snapped my image—
cheeks adolescent, blooming
among the japonica and banana plants

and it was today.

That picture, fading, hangs on the wall
of the big house where we once lived.
The painted doorknobs came from France.
During winter ten fireplaces were lit.

Now, on the other side of the green jalousie
a wedding party deflowers our lawn.
They're photographed as if they owned the place.
I grit my teeth and shuffle
out the back door as another group
of tourists is taken in
to hear the spiel of golden days:

hospitality, generals in gray,
family tradition—such shit!
Such heirs. Cruel drunks
and dreamy tarts. I sold
my childhood to pay for theirs.

Now, any evening, above the barges' moan
and cicadas' whine, giggles seep
from the old slave cabins.
"Guests of the Estate" mess up our beds,
leave dirty dishes for me to clean.
They loiter by the Coke machine all night,
cracking white-trash yankee jokes.

I turn the TV up loud,
polish my silver and smoke,
alone at the end of the way
in the old overseer's house.

Short History of a Woman with a Tattooed Scalp

1986
"Ain't no Georgia peaches
born in Vietnam,"
her high school president
scolds first day of class
when she shows up pretty
in a saffron skirt, her bangs
sprayed stiff into a wave.

That night she shaves it off.
The next morning skips class
to feel the needle's jag
in a parlor on Montgomery Street.
The pricked skin scrolls
like a lampblack fern
sprouting from her brain.

Her classmates gawk.
Matrons at the Oglethorpe Mall
glare over their shoulders
as she promenades past.
Her father speaks of shame.
Her mother shrugs and goes on
watching television.

1988
On St. Paddy's Day
a frat boy from Atlanta
soaks her with green beer.
A biker shoves her hard
onto the cobblestones.
All of Savannah seems intent
to rake her with its bile.

Some months later, she leans
against the lighthouse rail
on Tybee Island. Her hair
is growing out. Ahead,
the sea. Behind her,
the salt marshes like a map
of the Land of Always Lost.

1993
The first time that she makes love
is on her wedding day.
The soldier's chapped hands
clutch her skull.
He shudders as if starved.
"What's that under your hair?"
he asks. She whispers: "A scar."

Dog Eat Dog

(Covington, Kentucky, 1976)

Just look at her. When I come home
she's trashed. Sue's diapers stink
and I have to change them even though
I just got back from nine hours
in the paper mill and I need to puke
already. She lays the table—
why is there always shit stuck
in my fork when she says she takes hours
to clean the dishes? We shut up
and eat. She fiddles with her hair
and whispers and when I say, "What?"
she says, "Nothing." I change my shirt
and take off fast as I can go
down to the bar where—if people
are crocked—they still know a good joke
to pass the time until it's time
for sleep and work, and sleep and work.

*

I'm singing this Nugent song
every time Bill goes out
Dog Eat Dog
watching soaps
and drinking on the six-pack
I buy at the mini-mart
after Truth or Consequences
the baby's pulling pots and pans
from the cupboard
but I just rub the cool can

against my cheek
Dog Eat Dog
it sounds right
then baby howls
and I have to think about dinner
washing each dish careful
because Bill gets so mad
and out the kitchen window
cars are going somewhere
I'm trying to sing
but my tongue's swollen
and I've said it so many times
the words don't make sense at all

When I Saw the Swastika

inked into a black man's forehead

on the cover of a New York art magazine,
I thought of some big-eared dirt farmer

—first in his family to come to WVU—
his cock shriveling at the sight

of an enemy who had taken his place
in the Pantheon of Success.

Maybe the kid had just been jostled
in the hall by inner-city jocks

or had understood too clearly a gesture
of hands. These hollows bubble

with so many fundamental
particles of hatred, so many slogans

on which to slobber, it's no wonder
if he was frightened at the signs

of color confidently displayed,
if he retaliated in the ancient manner—

with this archaic symbol of good luck.

This Poem Is Not About Charleston, South Carolina

Not about the winter Sunday morning I went walking
by gaunt houses of pale pink and Charleston green,

shuttered, bricked and bolted,

laced with iron and mounted by airy cupolas,
not about my stroll along the battery, through flocks of
    pigeons

which settled in White Point Gardens like a lie.

Instead, this poem is a paean to my feet,
thanksgiving for my ankles, thighs and hips.

The church bells were only celebrating

my ascent from the cracked sidewalk,
the day was only made that I might glide past

the window boxes planted with geraniums and thyme.

Inner Ear Infection: Union City, Tennessee

I was watching the doctor's lips   something
    about wanting   to look deeper
when he left the room   I assumed it was time
    to get in my four-by-four   I played
the Haydn tape again loud   all the kids
    out at Reelfoot Lake   knew it was me
half-mile before I even parked   I was the biggest
    intellectual   in Obion County
and they were studying music   on an informal basis
    we drank enough sure   it was the Dixie beer
the kids always bought   maybe the doctor
    would find a cure   they talked
I explained the intricacies   of sonata-rondos
    inventions and returns   they chattered on
he had shone a light   in my ear
    what did he think he'd see   one
of the young ones vomited   allegro con spirito
    our conversation stretched   into morning
nodding vehemently   none of us
    had a clue   what was being said

17

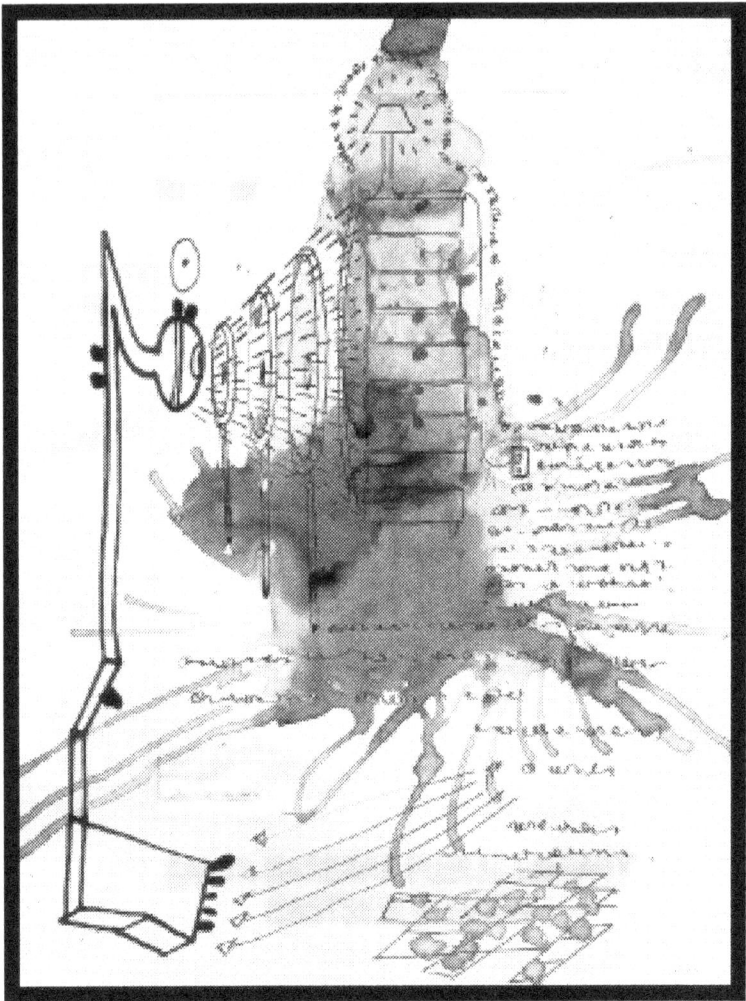

At the Grand Re-Opening of a Supermarket in Pompano Beach

Thick scent of jessamine, light rain
sparkling in the spotlight: perfect
night for a grand premier. Crowds—awed
by the spectacle—mince past the mincemeat,
the neon FRESH FRUIT signs. Unexpected
triangles of pink intersect
squares of aquamarine. Po-Mo?
Sure, but so much more. And what
museum of modern art is edible?

So tempting, in fact, is this display
that one old man ignores his years
of custom and, in front of a clerk,
plucks a green apple from the piles
and bites into its tart young flesh.
A drop of juice slides down his troughs
of skin, glistening in the glare
like some foresworn sparkle of lust.

Bay St. Louis

Above the mad whitecaps
My car creeps through the slapping rain,
   Along the concrete thread
Strung taut across Lake Pontchartrain.

   Water is the dominant
Sounded in morning's coastal tonic:
   A lazy swim, salty air.
The waves, womb-warm. The sun, laconic.

   Born again I was—
My thin white limbs washed free of need.
   I might have been a first
Promise, a new creature, a seed.

   Now, driving home, the clouds'
Drumming, the chorus in the air
   Proclaim the road need not
Run straight. There are exits everywhere.

True Love Apparent in Idabel, Oklahoma

Showers, they both think, looking
out the kitchen window. Wordlessly
he lays down Gin. She's up

then, making tuna fish sandwiches
and spooning in iced tea. He sets
out napkins and two plates.

The air conditioner hums, he hums
an oil-field ditty she will halt
midway, as usual. Later, they nap.

In 1947 she left, taking
their now distant son, and lived
with her sister in Ardmore. Eventually

and inevitably (it seemed to both)
she returned. It was equal, except
for the money, where she was.

He never looked up from his hunting
magazine as she hung up her dresses
and the child's knickers, cleaned

the little piles in the hall.
The moving from town to town continued,
chasing pools of underground crude.

His last job was here, so they stayed
through an eternity of Christmases,
an infinity of late afternoons....

Illegal Alien

The two worn twenties
he clutches in his pocket
are engines and
humming he softly
shuts the door
of his Hideaway Motel room.
First night in America,
he wants to see the place
so he strides
down Main Street, peeking
inside the Van Horn Diner,
nodding hello
to the *vaqueros* idling
outside.
       His legs
are pistons pushing
him past the sage,
which blows like clouds
toward the Wylie Hills,
until he stands so high
that he might be looking up
rather than down
on the dark valley,
so high
that each porch light
in West Texas
might be a star
in a constellation
no one has yet discovered.

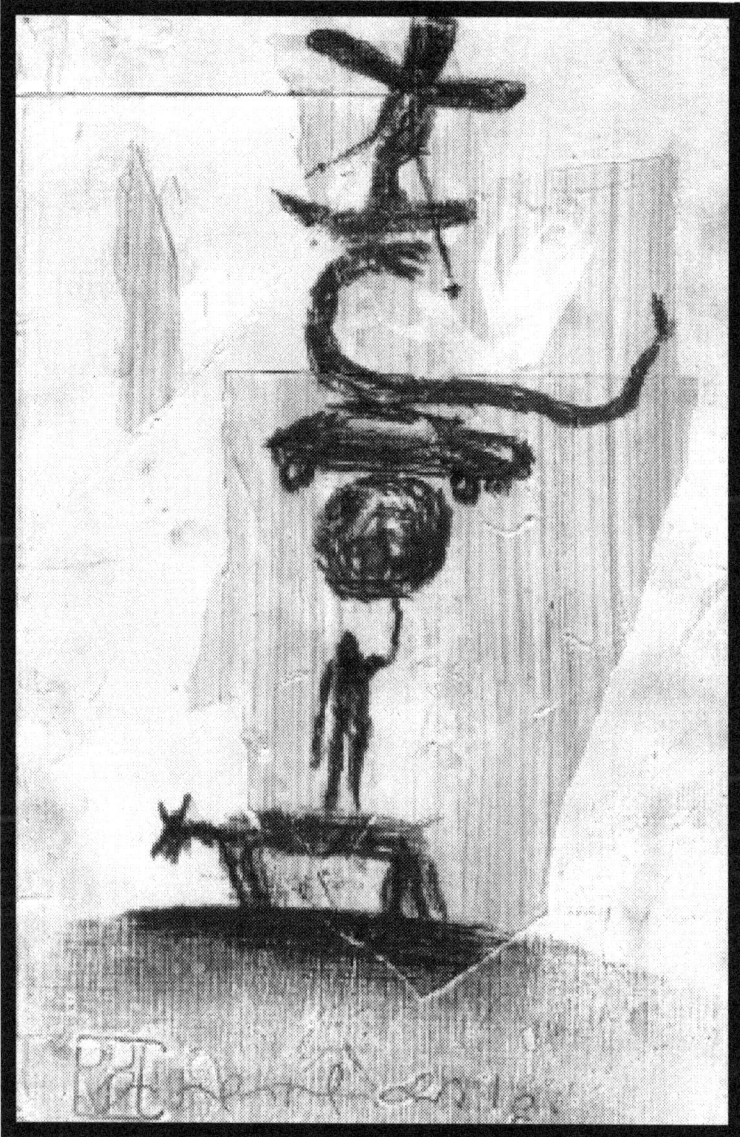

NORTHEAST

Taking the Kids to Washington, DC

We come bearing our state's nickname
on our license plates: Empire,
Pine Tree, Land of Opportunity.

In cars littered with travel games,
frantic wives page through guidebooks
as husbands, lost, demand

silence and directions.
Beaver, Badger, Volunteer,
here on The Mall we nuclear

families feel at home.
The monuments confirm what we had guessed,
that photographs don't lie,

the flag's still there.
We have to laugh at the Mint guide's,
"Sorry, no free samples,"

chuckle at the White House jokes,
beneficent because we know
that our vote counts.

We paid for these rockets
in the space museum, their needles
pointing to the Plexiglas sky.

Our grandfathers wrote the history books
one afternoon when they were bored.
Sunshine, Show Me, Lone Star, Hoosier,

Hawkeye, Blue Grass, Silver, Gem.
Declaration of Independence,
Zero Milestone,

Metro, Panda, Eternal Flame.
—*Shut up in the backseat*
or we're going home.

"Excuse Me, Is There a McDonald's in Your Historic Little Town?"

Damn right...but there wouldn't be,
if not for sacrifice
at The Peach Orchard,
The Wheatfield,
Little Round Top and Spangler's Spring.

No RVs would come.
No banners would fly.
No grandchildren clambering over cannons
or grandsires hunting
for souvenirs in our quaint shops.

A traveler passing by
would circumvent Main Street.
The only nightlife, a four-by-four
tearing down the county road,
one stray dog barking in the woods.

So don't give me that War Is Useless
smirk when you're starving
for a Big Mac after touring
the well-kept remnants
of our bloody battlefields all day.

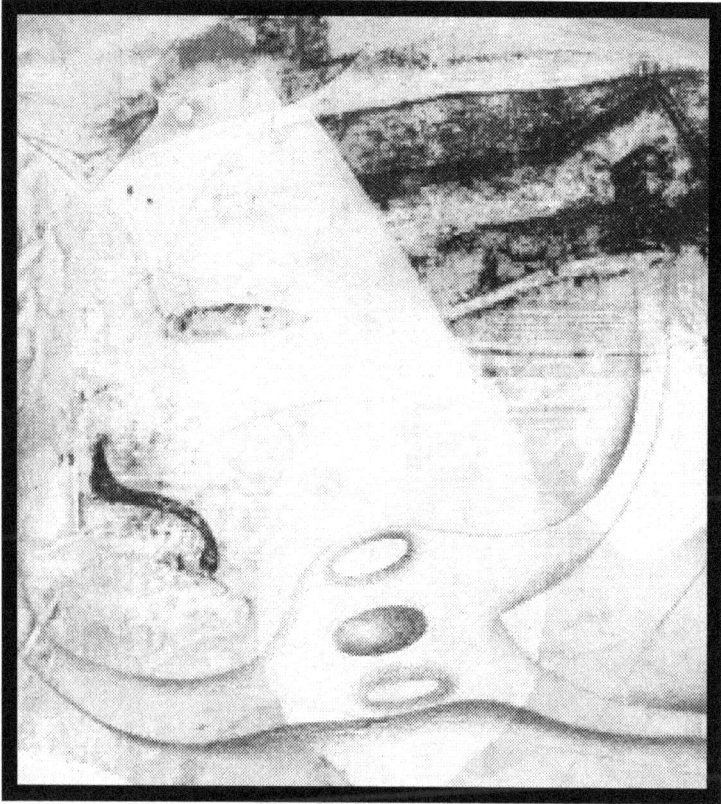

Annapolis, 1971

Carpe diem, man,
she'd said that morning.
Get me out of Baltimore.

What the hell, right?
We'd almost been married once
and still slept together on holidays.

I lay her out in the back seat
like a corpse—thought she'd be down
for hours—but by Glen Burnie

she's awake and swallowed a pill
and then it doesn't stop:
My jaws are tight mugglehead

I mean one get-down too many
don't suit my second brain
and I'm not talking some lazy jag

I'm hooked sucker monolithic...
We end up on King George Street,
but of course that's right across

from the Academy and we haven't walked
five yards before First Lieutenant Hardass
starts nuzzling up to her,

Hey, babe. Wanna party?
in that drawl that makes you think
every man in uniform was raised

on the same Georgia pig farm. I try
to nudge him off but he wants
to fight a freak, and all the time

she's going on, *Stroke your own lizard*
dirthole no more mazola parties
no more mix the peanut butter

no more furburger for you...
Thank God a church bell chimes—
swabby steers back for duty

and we find a café near City Dock.
Suddenly, it's quiet.
Just coffee, she mumbles

before dropping off to sleep.
Smell of boiled crabs,
fried chicken. I would have split

if she hadn't started snoring,
if I hadn't realized
I didn't love her anymore.

New Haven Predicament

Publish or Paris...
            —Overheard at Yale

My Department Chair was clear.
One review a week,
One article a month,

One book a year,
Or he would have no other choice:
Banishment.

But day and night
My cursor blinked
On an otherwise empty screen.

Former colleagues
Wrote bitterly from exile.
In letters of exquisite tediousness

They lamented the lovers on every park bench,
The drag shows and light opera,
Toy sailboats in the *Jardin du Luxembourg*,

Public embraces in noisy coffee houses,
Fine wine, fresh bread,
Strong cigarettes and pungent cheese.

I knew I wouldn't last a week.
My office hours were as lonely
As winter in the *Bois de Boulogne*.

"*À bientôt,*" sniped a rival Romanticist
As I tossed out my *PMLA*s.
Someone stamped my passport, "No Return."

Before the plane had even landed
I heard laughter, singing, moaning.
Accordion music like a funeral organ.

After Learning She Is Pregnant

She's sweating in the elevator,
going down with a woman
who wears rosewater and a man
who stares absently
at her flat stomach. The car stops
at every other floor.
                    On Fifth Avenue,
two yuppies fight
for a cab. A beggar shouts,
"Hey, lady. Hey, LADY!"
The music of bells chimes
behind the window of a Mercedes,
and she falls
                    against a parking meter
like a farmer
leaning on her hoe,
listening to "Beautiful Dreamer"
played off-key on the carillon
of a small college
far across the ripening fields,
miles and miles away.

Security Parking, Hoboken

You never want to live without it again.
Over are the days
of leaving your car in the alley,

in the lot next to the liquor store
so many dark blocks away.
You wonder how you ever stood

the uncertainty,
how you ever made it without the assurance
of a solid iron gate

sliding shut between you
and the angry foreign voices
plotting against your return.

Your new whitewashed building is as beautiful
and impenetrable
as the White Swan Castle at Hemiji.

Pious as a shogun,
you are free
to contemplate the blossoming trees

in your walled garden,
wholly unresponsive to any spirit
but your own.

Acrostic / Anagrams: New Hampshire

Near where a wisp of smoke
eases into the wash of ashen sky,
we whisper of fresh harm skirted anew.

Here beneath the snow-wrapped birch and fir
arise questions we can't answer;
maps of awe appear,
praise for warmth and wine—then
sharp phrases (too harsh for seraphim)
hamper our walk: you halt
in mid-stride, wish violently that I would not
rehash the past, remind me it's much
easier to neglect than sin. Amen.

Elegy: Murderkill

In this grove of lindens
we figured out the easy ones,
"Heart of Gold"
and "Like a Hurricane."
That was something we had in common.
And we could piss our last names
in the snow.
                But college,
it fades. Cheap beer,
greaser boots clicking on pavement,
his owlish eyes bright in early evening:
"Wilmington is so dead."
Being born in the second
smallest state, that was something
else—
            and a microdot
of garbage windowpane, dead whales
beached on the riverbank,
cattle wandering untended
down Lancaster Avenue.
What visions of the plague we shared
ten years ago.
               Friends,
"for truth," but he changed his name,
took a job in California, plucked me
before leaving like catgut,
and I'm sorry if he's dead,
but I wasn't about to ask
for a handful of ashes
to toss into a stream the Dutch named
three hundred years ago.
I wasn't about to jump into the Delaware Bay.

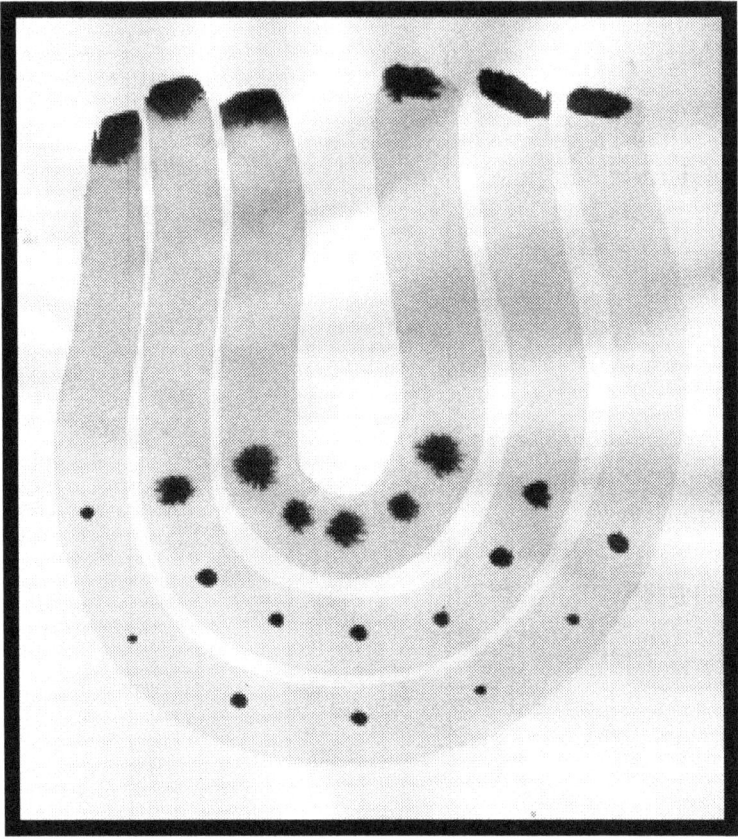

Allen Ginsberg in Thoreau's Maine Woods

Cold, soaking, wrapped in wet wool, I lean
    towards sputtering camp fire,
        tin mug of coffee
in chapped red hands, burrs in socks,
        runny nose, Heaven clapped
to forehead. Buddha-memories, Blake painting,
    stoned on wildflowers in thick pine forest—
Skullcap, Meadow-Rue, St. John's Wort,
        Black Snake-
    Root, Common Virgin's Bower.

        No virgin, I
mind-breathe native hymns, Om Ah Hum.
      Nasal strain of our guide,
    Savage nobler than any Captain Amerika—
shrewd chants, not trivial Republocrat
    Wall Street Journal radio exchange songs,
        but Tremors, War, Sadness
& Love Lost on banks of black northern rivers—
    Umbazookskus, Chesuncook, Caucomgomoc.

Comely Animals howl, mad promenade in Bohemian
    Ktaadn night. Lynx, Sable, Hedgehog,
      Beaver, Otter, Moose
gulp lungfuls of Alder scent, sweet Choke-Cherry
     & Mountain Holly,
furious fur tossed towards bitch-goddess Diana—
       myriad paws waving at white orb, sole
    solace in this wretched, lovely, pitch-blind,
      viscous wilderness of screams.

Maxine in Her Cups

They want to feed me pablum here;
I'd rather have a drink, my dear.
Fetch me the whiskey from your purse—
I *know* it's there—quick now, I'll curse.
Much better. It's hard inside this bright
bare place to remember how twilight
seeped slowly into my house on hot
evenings. (I'll take another shot.)
The doctors experiment on me,
though what they'll learn from a ninety-three
year old mind, I haven't a clue.
"Why not slice my brain open? Do
you think you'll find my life in there?
No sir!" They smile. I've become air
already to the sons-of-whores.
—Quiet: they hide behind the doors.
(And one more drop...if you don't mind.)
At least one of my kin is kind.
Would you like to share some laughs?
Hand me that book of photographs
and postcards there. Look. Belgium, France.
Louie sent them, my first romance.
Nineteen-twelve. I was sixteen.
We'd dance and he'd whisper obscene
words in my ear. There's Catherine,
your great-great aunt. A weird woman.
The Witch of Hazen's Notch. She swept
people's houses all day, but kept
her own a mess. She loved black cats,
went shopping in a pointed hat.
Oh, this one I want you to keep.

A group of us standing knee-deep
in the Lamoille. Our arms are crossed,
our grins, cock-eyed...we were half-sauced.
Louie's arm is round my waist.
Ages ago, but I still can taste
his sweat. Mary has such a stiff
grin, Harold, such arms. We look as if
we could turn the world on its head.
Lay eyes on them: all dead, all dead.

Antique

Her grandfather poured Amaretto
into elaborately engraved tumblers,
lit our Turkish cigarettes
and withdrew from the parlor.
By this we were to understand
that she and I were through.
She seemed slightly surprised
(I'd learned in the six months past
that Newport matters
are often decided by one man),
but her recovery time was quick.
A collection of obsolete wind instruments
hung on the wall, and we glanced
up at them as we mumbled our accusations:
desultory...impulse...flimflam.
Whispering through the lattice,
a sea breeze turned the yellowed pages
of an ancient book of botanical drawings,
its Latin ablur. How damned silly!
I kept thinking through the perfumed haze,
yet it hurt just the same.
Resinous and opaque,
our parting drifted above
the African masks, the Edo screens
of peacocks and courtesans
with hair the color of oats at harvest.
It's certainly not worth preserving, she said,
flicking ash into her empty snifter.
Of course not, I agreed,
though I could imagine someone much like myself
wading across the nearby shoal

from the depths of the past and gone,
into the shallow present.

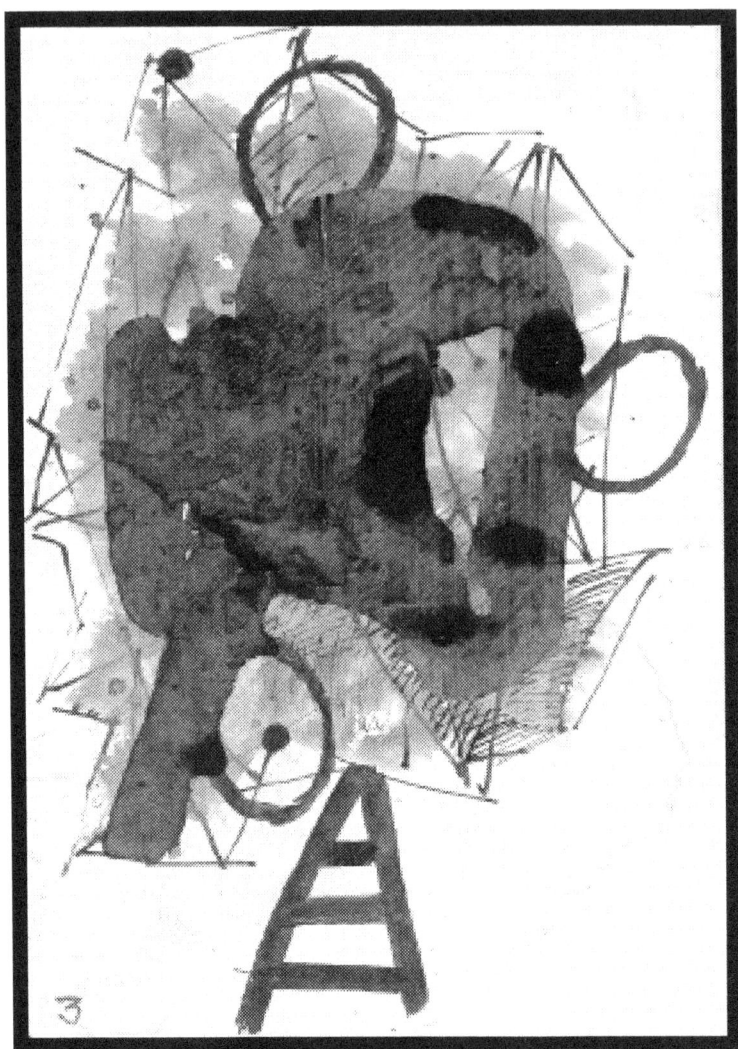

Emerson: Concord, 1882

Come in, sit down. I fear I must have missed
Your name. My memory has quite vanished.
So many used to visit me—Heavens,
The talk!—but I have lost my gift for thought.
You wish to watch my genius mend decay,
But you will be roundly frustrated, sir:
Nature's decay it is that mends genius.
At least we have a lovely April day.
What is that bird out the window? a lark?
Its song, though dulcet-toned, seems touched with grief.
I'm but a passing naturalist, as good...
Someone will testify.
                              Ah, was only
Last week I walked with him through cathedrals
Of mighty pines. We must have spent a year
Camping in woods, at night reading God's palm.
Instructive chiromancy. My Scottish
Friend—the dour, brilliant one—had learned,
Had he been there, the end, if hard, is just
And often beautiful.
                              Why, yesterday
I was in England hiking down the moors.
We'd gone to see a man I admired
As a youth—he who embraced revolution
Then took refuge behind his garden gate—
But he had nothing new to say, nothing.
I can't abide a mind that's fossilized.

Let us have something warm to sip, perhaps
That drink that stains one's teeth—tea, yes!—I feel
Lucid today, more than I have in years.

Lately my thoughts evaporate like rain
In June. Shakespeare's a jumbled dream. And yet
You wonder at my calm visage so close
To death? It's because I have slipped the knot
Of mere mortality. Sometimes I think,
When wandering, I am already passed
Into the over-soul. In this study,
Which should be so familiar, I lose
All trace of time. The walls, the clock,
The very book I'm holding in my hands,
Are ciphers beckoning: I swim into
Their caves. Ages pass, till my daughter comes,
As she is now, with the drink that stains one's teeth.

Forgive the mess, my house, alas burned down
This morning. Fortunately, my good friends
Have rebuilt it this afternoon, though smoke
Still lingers in my nose (later we'll sneak
Outside for a cigar) and my fingers
Are charred.
                    Darkness and light. My brain, that bee,
Always in haste from thought to thought, takes flight
Now at the slightest shift of wind. Your eyes
Seem sockets only—strange illusion!—please
Excuse me, I must go upstairs to rest.
Sweet water, sleep, I crave a healing draught.
Here is the door—I'm addled now.
                                        So still?
Is it illness, my friend, that makes you keep
Your seat? Ellen! This gentleman is sick.
—Dear girl, he's there...or was. He must have left
When I was in the hall. How impolite.
Yes, yes, I'll be up presently.
                                —My God,
Where did you hide, weird sir, to reappear
Like this? You'll come again, and soon? Just so,

46

I value visitors. But please come well
Announced next time, that I may know your name.

MIDWEST

Mary Ellen Baker Muses While Listening to Sojourner Truth's Speech at the Ohio Women's Rights Convention of 1851

An air of confrontation, the rustle
Of cambric muslin, fans stirring the heat.
She strides in, queenly; the few men make a bustle—
"The Libyan Sibyl." We're all on our feet.
Her knobby hands wave a white cane, a white
Turban spirals from her head. Her face is flint,
But her voice warm milk. (They say a fight
Broke out once when some cocksure, prominent
Citizens declared she was a man. She bared
Her breasts, shouted, "I might have suckled one
Of yours!") Now, eyes glistening, huge nostrils flared,
She pours it on, acrid and saccharin:
"I could work and eat as much as any man,
Then dance at night, and ain't I a woman?"

She's wild. I think I would not ask her home,
As Mrs. Stowe is said to do. Enos
Would not approve—at all. That man, he's sewn
Me in his house (he thinks), and yet he knows
Nothing of my life, not even where I am.
I bake his bread and stew his meat. "Too much
Spice" is his thanks. Next meal, I'll use marjoram
Enough to sweeten his sour smiles. A crutch
Is what he is. But Sojourner's alone.
Why not me? Why not? My mother, the child,
Nowhere to go. On my modest tombstone
They'll write (liars!), "Faithful, Loving, and Mild."
In my crinoline I curtsey to each man,
But inside I curse, for I, too, am a woman.

Home

These brown Dakota fields are strange,
although I've made my bed since second grade
within eye's reach of that farm girl
who's plump now with our bastard child.
No matter that I bent
                              a blue-jeaned knee
upon her porch and spent my bank money
to buy a ring,
                    she was fierce,
never wanted "this sort of trouble."
She planned to make me pay.
I pulled down the brim of my work cap
so she wouldn't see my eyes.
                                        "Passion
is no virtue in a young man," the preacher,
her father, intoned. He had land, too,
that needed working, jingled the change
in his pocket: "No one said life is easy.
You start tomorrow morning
at four."
            "Eventually the heart
sleeps with the head,"
Father declares. And Mother sighs,
"This is how families begin:
                                    not always in joy."

Meet Me in St. Louis

i.

The people in the alley wore ripped pin-stripped suits
and made the sign of the cross to passersby. Hornets,
too, lived there, swarming over the garbage. She,
however, was being played in high rotation
on MTV. Once a day he rose from his pallet
of packing crates and newspapers and limped up Canal
to watch the storefront televisions blare her hit.
The other dancers wore leather, but she was all white.
And they were so nasty with their bump-bend-and-grind
while she was angelic. *Come unto me*, her eyes
invited. Blood passing from raised veins at the Red Cross
blenched his brain of all but her. Unharbored, he
shot a loaded sailor, seized his roll and shared
the stake with his alley friends. A big winner,
somewhere, the sailor must have been. It was an hour
of unbounded promise and mutual blessing.

ii.

A disappointing follow-up. A child. Not the skids,
naturally, but not what she'd hoped. Three years later
she had a home, a husband and a weekend job
at a "nice" place, singing for conventioneers
at her husband's uncle's lounge, The Gateway to the West.
Meanwhile, he sputtered up from New Orleans—Natchez,
West Memphis, carrying a well-thumbed memory
like a book of verse he'd forgotten how to read. One night
he sees the *Post-Dispatch*, her picture, those glowing
blue eyes. He cleans his nails, though what can she say?
He knots his tie. The rented room's a wreck.

How can she bear him here? He coughs up confusion
like phlegm, but still his lungs are full of something foul.
Outside the lounge he hears her voice, flattering yet sweet,
"Don't tell me the lights are shining / Any place but there."
He waits. He wants to wait always. Just outside the door.

Petoskey

They were two men
of great natural cowardice.

Inevitably, fate revealed the flaw
in their otherwise perfect plan.

They tried to hire a boat
but the bay was solid ice.

The Mackinaw bridge was closed
and a front was on the way.

Not to mention **FBI** from Detroit,
organized crime from Toledo.

They sat in a diner
listening to skiers brag of recent runs.

Crunching tire chains in the parking lot
might mean any of several things.

"The airport," one suggested.
"If there is one," replied the other.

Instead they found a boarding house.
HO E CO K D ME LS, read the sign outside.

Their breath sparkled in the moonlight.
"Don't even think of moving," a voice commanded.

They stood there.
Petrified.

Thing

"I farm the land," he tells her in a bar,
mud on his stubbled cheek and his Cat cap.

She's a waitress: "I *was* headed out west.
My rides gave out and now I'm stuck."
                                North Platte,
NE: Friday night. Trucks pull under grain
elevators, idle, their drivers spitting
in mounds of hulls. "I work an honest week,"
he says. "On weekends I cut loose."
                                "Me, too."

Her place is close. Her dog. The windows shut.
He pants for breath, but draws in only dust,
leaving the blanket littered with thistles.

It grows, their thing, predictably—a crop
that's known to turn a small profit then rot
(on time, he hopes). She doesn't seem to care.

Those months, twelve-pack late nights. Her soap plots,
        girls
at work knocked up, her rent. His aching back,
his pick-up truck, a stamp for duck season.

Toward the end they take the thing outside.
When cottonwood shadows stretch across the soil
baked and gray and shooting up with corn,
the green lies rustle off her tongue and plop
into the gray canal.
                        He finds them whole,

years later, still silky and still husk-hard.
Sliced open with a knife, the seeds burst forth.
Vegetable. Flourishing. Unmarked by time.

Pottawatomie Creek

When I woke to the cold hand
on my shoulder, I thought God had come
to take me for swiping
Isaiah's peppermints.
A bushy-bearded man grunts,
Outside.
        Quick now, son,
Father whispers. Oil lamp
makes the walls shiver like grass.
T' others had hands on heads.
Isaiah pulled on his boots.
No need for that,
Man says.
         Then we're all in the dark.
It was May, time for summer work.
Man starts talking.
His voice is beautiful,
like the Preacher's in Mobile.
Points his rifle, says,
               Lord,
forgive these Southerners
strayed so very far
from your Word. It is like a sickness
come upon them and they cannot
now be cured.
         Two of these
is only boys, Father says.
And they will grow to men,
says he.
        Uncle rushed forward
then fell to the sod.

Father held my hand.
My friend, we also antislavery.
It was a lie, he cursed for slaves
walking behind the plow.
                               His hand
slips from mine.
The man who works for us began to run
then isn't running. Isaiah knelt,
crying. Please, mister. I hate Kansas,
my brother and me both do.
                               Gun coughs
again and I was left alone. Boy,
he says, not talking to me,
looking toward Orion's belt,
I will enter history.
And you, he murmurs, his voice
is water,
                you will be forgotten.

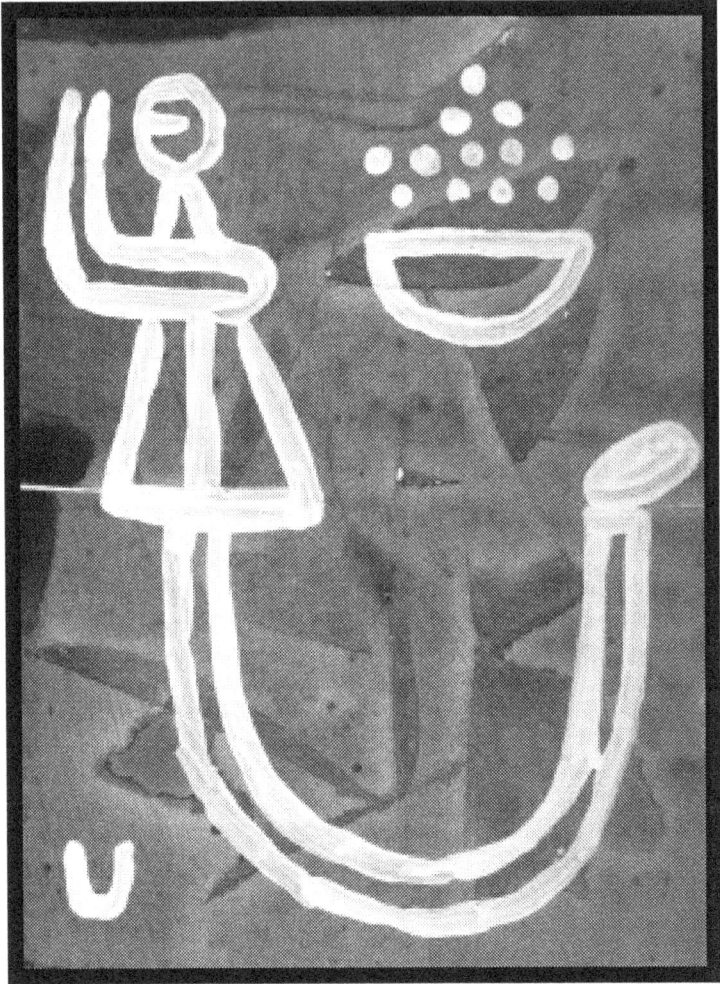

Miscarriage

Through with his daily lessons at the Academia,
he steps into the cobblestone street,
breathes deeply the smoke from fatty *churros*
burning in grease. Three black Mercedes
creep uphill toward the cathedral.
He drops a fifty peso coin in a withered
bodiless hand.
                In Minneapolis,
his wife is vomiting. Her chin
on cold porcelain. The smell of toothpaste
and urine. *It's not time,* she thinks,
hurrying through the snow in bedroom slippers,
met at the hospital by rough unfamiliar hands.
Her doctor is out of town.
                      That night,
there is celebration in the square.
Toothless old women applaud the children
brave enough to touch the catherine wheel
spinning red and green and white.
She'd like this, he thinks, snapping
a picture to send with his next note.
                        She grips
the nurse's arm, seeing nothing but lights.
Everywhere, lights.

A Plan

We're leaving De Kalb at one-thirty a.m.,
   my girlfriend and I, after drinking, like, eight
Inky Caps at Trino's Lounge, and I tell her,
   "We're driving to Chicago, you plump, nimble
piece of sass, and don't say a word against it,"

but she's asleep, snoring like the yellow-dog
   her father always was, so I keep talking:
"Look, just don't label me. My innards
   are my own. I don't come from some Palatine
pseudo-intellectual tradition, but I know

what I'm saying. You don't have to initiate *me*."
   All the while the *cuhhhhh* coming from her throat
is making me cotton-mouthy, but I don't want to stop
   even long enough for a drive-thru Coke, I'm going
too fast, past Aurora and Naperville

and Downer's Grove, then I'm barreling down the Ike,
   Cicero on my right, Loretto Heights Hospital
on the left. "You know, one percent of all the homicides
   in the world are committed within one square mile
of that place," I tell her, repeating a factoid

that may or may not be correct. Pause.
   "Doesn't that scare you?" Pause, then gurgle-snort.
"Rosalind, I have to say it, sometimes I feel so...well,
   ultracentrifugal. Do you know what I mean?"
In response, she coughs up a little ball of spit

that rests in the corner of her mouth. "I mean,
    I feel as though I've entered a sort of spiritual
torrid zone. The social registry is no longer an issue.
    A reputation sweet as attar is out of the question.
Rosalind, the desert's in here. I'm thrashing

for meaning and you're rasping like a file against steel.
    Listen: my throat is *dry*." She gasps a little.
Smiles, I guess—it's more a sign of plastered trust,
    then turns her head toward the window and drifts off.
And that's it. I can already visualize it.

The Ike peters out under the Post Office,
    but I run all the red lights on West Congress,
drive right through the Fountain, through Grant Park
    and smash through Lake Shore Drive right into
the goddamn lake itself, into that place

where every watery yearning is quenched, a great big
    sopping Valhalla for all the hayseed screw-offs
like me, all the ill-starred couples fated to vanish
    into the drink because one was sleeping off
a jag and the other, by God, had a plan.

Council Bluffs, 1959

The B & O nearly snatches
His sleep but it's brief

Only ten cars tonight and he drifts

Back to his favorite dream
Himself magician

At a fancy dinner party

Vanishing napkins, floating knives
An affair of nimble fingers

Hours of satin wizardry

He's sawing an assistant in half when
A cattle car rattles though early dawn

The lowing wakes him

Bound for blood
He half rises from his cot

And already her soft skin

Is cold gunmetal
Her sweat tastes of light oil

Tonight he'll make her see the picture
Rio Bravo is still playing

Across the river in Omaha

Expectant Father: Bad Trip

The beginning is always low comedy: a fork
in the toaster, every bone in the skeleton plain
as clear water. Monona, Mendota—either
way wet. What follows? The pleasure of sleeping deeply
and a lifetime of annealing the brittle shard
of guilt. Each new decision is as irrelevant

as the dead moths caught inside a porch light's globe,
so that when Sweet Sixteen comes, the party's already
over. Festal? Well, picture a guy drinking gin
in a cheap hotel, listening to the *Elvis Christmas
Album* in July. And why not, with that voice, stern
yet avuncular, blaring over the P.A., "Fall

on your knees before this banquet: saltines and tuna
and chalices of grape Kool-Aid." Duty is stitched
like a nickname on the Man's breast. After all, it's
a father's job to give birth. Remember, Zeus ate
all that was left of his son Dionysus, the heart,
and, nauseous, spewed a perfect image of himself.

Television Tower

For those few
who have
breached security
and managed
to ascend
the tallest
structure
in North America—
2000 feet
above the wheat-
grass and rye
and sugarbeets,
above
the glory hole
of Devils Lake,
sandy rivers,
spattered barns—
the great surprise
is how little
you can see.
Oh there's Grand
Forks, Fargo but
emptiness
takes up a lot
of space.
The shades
of Eric Severaid,
Lawrence Welk
and Peggy Lee
have long since
dried to dust,

for ambition
always bolts
with the hard
Plains wind,
southwesteast,
remote from home
in a blizzard
of no regrets.

Phillis Wheatley in East Chicago

She leaves the market with a cold R.C.
and a pack of Kool Lights. Two centuries
of persecution have steered her from God,
or at least from the Methodists' pale fraud,
and she shakes her head sadly at the group
lingering on a storefront church's front stoop.
Due north she walks, up Indy Boulevard
past the young men on corners, poor and bored
but learning. Her new shoes tap a sure beat—
weak-strong, weak-strong. The rhythm in her feet
is constant as her own calm pulse. She stepped
just once, accidentally but stiff-lipped,
through a hole in history. That damp, cheap room
in Boston became so heavy with gloom
it sank into itself and pulled her along,
leaving a fake to fill the grave. The song
she sings now is fleeting as bus exhaust,
wordless as her asthmatic cough—and lost,
again, on all who can't redeem the norm,
those who don't see that function follows form.

WEST

How I Won the Indian Wars

From Bear River
to White Bird Canyon
to Camas Meadows,
I slaughtered the s.o.b.s.
Don't ask what names
they called themselves.
I didn't. It was enough
that they were there,
ready to fight.
I had rank and rotgut
and maybe a division
of cavalry somewhere—
who knows
what rifle smoke can hide?
Sure, even before
the last one dropped
like a flushed quail,
I guessed generations
would condemn my enterprise,
but I said: *Shit,*
when they're cozy
in their cabins
and know the only whistle
at dusk is winter wind,
then I'll be their silent hero,
at ease in the mud of history,
chewing on my plug of twist.

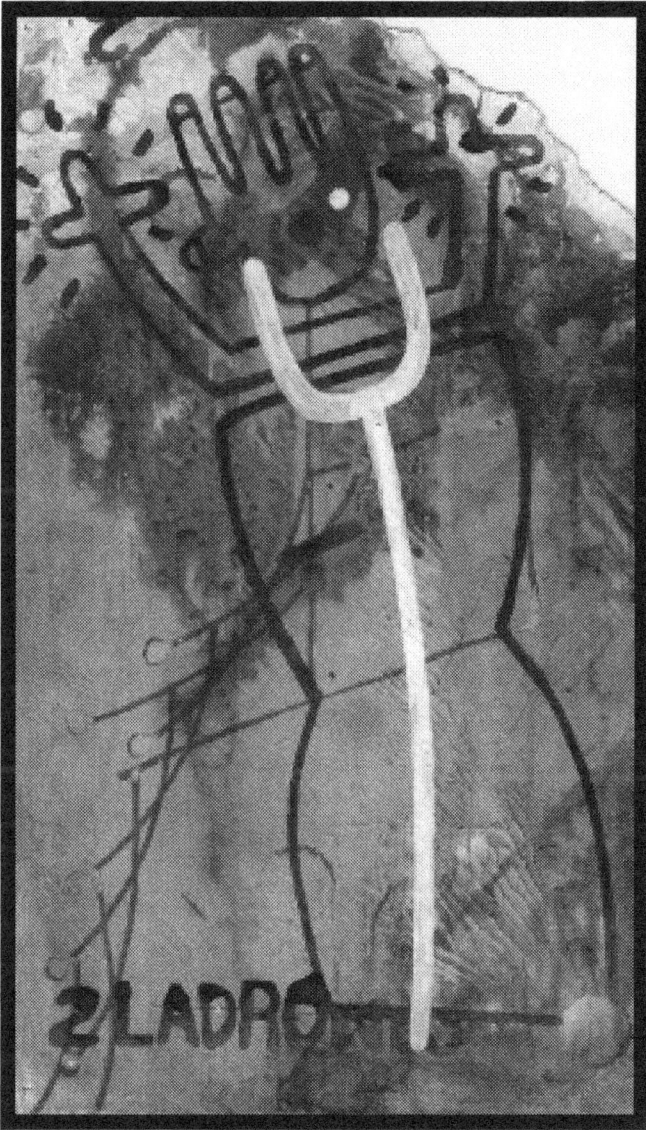

Portland

Like bleach through cloth

the wind penetrates his skin
and bleeds the warmth away

Kicking through piles of wet leaves

he hurries from the bus stop
grips tight his thin winter coat

with fingers chaffed from washing pots and pans

There's no tunneling a wish down
into this frozen hardpan so he prays

his breath wreathing upward

will drive off the Northwest cold
and coil around his family

like a snake guarding a temple door

For this he traded the grace of Hue
Skinhead blows

to jaw and ribs

Three room apartment
in a complex that stinks

more than the River of Perfumes

Uncle and aunt sleeping in the living room
Cousin curled up in the hall

Quietly he hangs

his coat and brews a pot of tea
pulling the kettle from the stove

just before it screams

Folly

On the Washington side of the Columbia River,
poured in concrete, Stonehenge stands.

Some Anglophile millionaire
(with too much time before he died)

standardized the circle,
smoothed the rocks' rough sides.

It doesn't work of course.
The vernal equinox might as well not come

for all the stars would show a man simple enough
to try and tell them from within that perfect band.

No hippies are arrested for tripping after hours,
no sacrifices are performed.

Summer evenings find only locals,
tippling wine coolers from vast Igloos.

How is it then that householders across the gorge
emerging into the violet dusk

claim to see evidence
of a new civilization springing up,

complete with absolute ideals
and gods still young enough to hold a grudge?

Suburban Ghosts

Through rustling palm leaves,
past tinkling wind chimes,
over the rippling swimming pools,
from the desert they come.

They shimmer like forbidden tobacco smoke
caught for an instant in porch lights,
cast dim reflections
in sliding glass doors.

They've come back to question loved ones
or whisper anamneses through the night—
here where they were happier,
death distant as headlines.

The red-haired girl across the street,
murdered by a motorcycle gang,
curls in the ivy, dreams
of squealing down the hill on her bike.

The hardware salesman next door
fondles his Siamese cat,
wife reading in the bedroom,
up late again on a work night.

And the newly-dead bishop,
famed for his benevolence and probity,
turns the Provo sky red with woe,
flickers late night TV shows

as he circles his comfortable ward,
searching every fragrant pantry
for the body someone hacked in parts,
without which he cannot seek the sky.

Rocky Mountain Women's Studies

Glenda: Fort Collins, 1968

My paper was called "The Heirs of Patriarchal
Domination." He told me, that night, I'd said
"hairs" all through it and he had thought of mine—
on my head, under my arms, between my legs.
This was after the reception where he'd spoken well
and wisely of lesbians and feminists.
Too much chablis. A Virginia Woolf poster
in his room. Candles and, I thought, respect. No.
When it—yes, *it*—was done, he mumbled, "Thanks,"
and fell asleep. I went home and revised
parts of my essay from experience.

Winifred: Boulder, 1973

I was eight months pregnant when he received
the call: a one semester research grant
to work in France. I told him, "Go," a gift
of wifely sacrifice I knew he'd refuse.
The day our son was born, a postcard came
from Lourdes: "The water's great. Wish you were here."
All right, he's young, ambitious, wasn't much
for kids. He did the dishes, cleaned the house.
Still, I tell you this—apparently
it's not so obvious—a man should not
be free with vows he will not keep, lest he
be ready to pay through the teeth. The house
is bare; I've sent my things to...let him guess.
The window frames a surge of peaks: cold, cold.

Jennifer: Pueblo, 1986

I took pity on him, I guess. Tragic
and misunderstood, that's how he came across.
You saw right though the act, of course. Only
his transparency made you want to help.
God! Do we ever grow up? Is life
a term of childcare, oblivious
to the selfishness it succors? He cooed
all night, resting his head on my breast. "Father
of Lies" I named him to my friends. He plays
with history; like Herodotus, the story
is his. Jobs, though, are hard to find. I need
the recommendation he'll have to give me now.

Michael: Denver, 1991

A hypocrite? I guess I am. I took
what I could get and criticized the world
that countenanced my theft. Ah, but I love
looking them over—their sleek, curving necks,
the unconscious grace with which they take plates down
from the shelf. Women are not *objets d'art*,
I know, I've written it many times myself,
but I stand and stare, a gallery patron,
and covet and am lost. Colleagues cried foul
when the Dean—golf chum, college buddy, a man—
appointed me Chair. My work was impeccable,
my life suspect. I ask, "Which matters more?"
These days, young women wander earnestly
to my briar-scented, book-lined den, and know
before they've left I am a fake. I smoke
through the nose, smile, and laud *The Second Sex*.

Watching a Full Moon Rise Above Scapegoat Mountain

—after Li Po

Sex
has brought me
nothing
but sorrow.

I prefer drinking
and the company
of large dogs.

Population Centers of Wyoming

Another lunar month.
Snow.
Encampment barren as a monastery.

Then a single whoop
at the hundredweight clouds
from some bored cowpoke's pistol.

Every river glacified
to its source.

In Cheyenne alleys
weather-hardened derelicts whisper,
"Famine?"

But, no, the general store
is open during blizzards,
there is still cooking coming
from the homespun housewives

whose wedding gowns are folded and stashed
in Etna's frost-riven basements,
in Eden's fossilized portmanteaux.

New Frontiers

Deming, New Mexico

There ought not to be
any faith left,

boxed in this last refuge

of American dreams—
aluminum house trailers

guarded by slat fences

too low to keep out cats
or neighborhood kids.

But the defiant

bumperstickers proclaim,
Tough Times Pass

Tough People Last,

dry hearts unfolding
like desert flowers

on the wrong side of the tracks,

expectant stalks thrust
toward the sliver of a moon.

Kin Song in L.A.

All these people here, and no one will be
a friend. I *admire* them, too—their just-right hair
and skins. I would take second seat gladly
in a pair, but they seek out each other's fair
faces. I'm different so I must be dumb.
Just yesterday a boy called me an ass.
My equation was slightly off. I felt so numb.
The teacher glared. I will not pass his class.

In Pusan, I won all the choice awards,
was thought to be merry and somewhat droll.
My parents beamed as they sent me toward
What they supposed was every young man's goal.

But these strangers curse the dirty, boding air
and are rewarded for their foreign prayer.

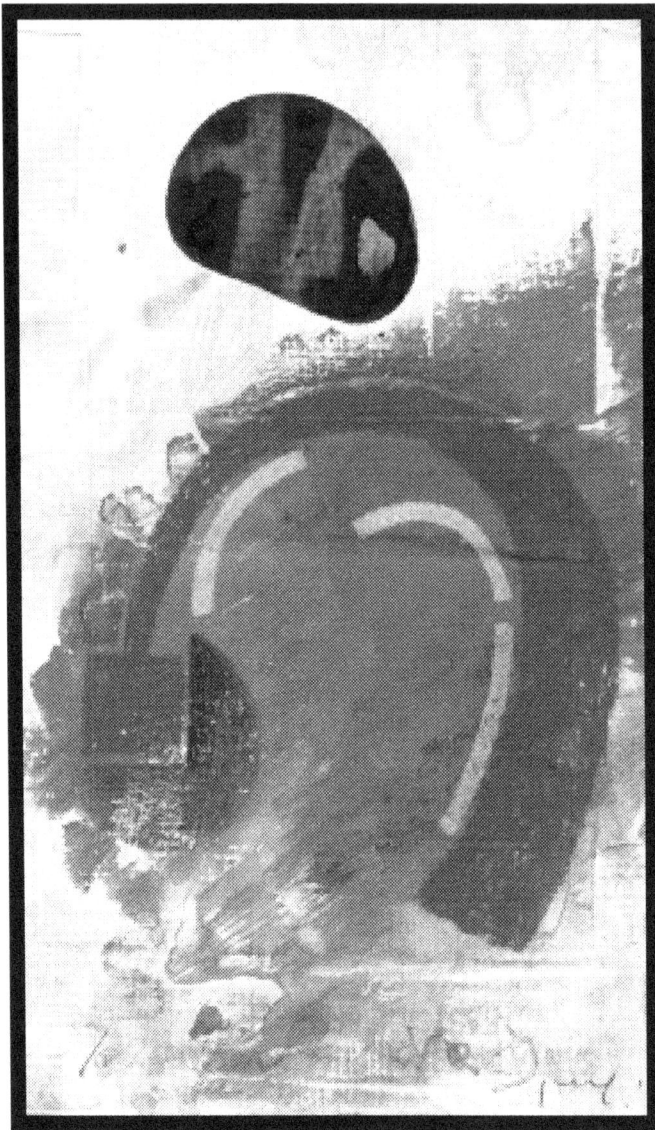

The Silver City Motel

In Nevada, things
blossom only once.
In the gray room

she unknots
her halter top,
spears his chest

with a fingertip.
Outside in the dust,
semis scrape gears.

Stiffly, he enumerates
the reasons he can't
bud. She scraps

the evening, goes
for planter's punch.
I should be devastated,

he's thinking
when she zips her purse.
Yet even as the door

swings softly shut
he can still count
two good things:

Carson City's just
down the road, and
her skin was worn

smooth as the bark
of a thousand year old
bristlecone pine.

Taxonomy

Camping out once in the Sand Tank Mountains
while working on my ethno-botany,
I woke at dawn to tires crunching gravel.

Two 4 x 4s jammed on their brakes. A man
was pushed into the dust. Quiet. Hedgehog
cactus bloomed carmine. A lizard froze

on the feathered branch of a Palo Verde tree.
Then four cowboy boots were kicking his groin.
No noise but one goldfinch, the man's mute grunts.

A hot wind shook the pink pentstemon flowers.
When they drove away I helped him up. We hiked
the mile to my car. His teeth were rotten, hands

cracked. He laughed, "I deserve it. I'm a cheat.
But, boy, will my balls be blue in the morning."
I dropped him off in Gila Bend, then drove

back to Phoenix, wrote up my logs, fired
a joint. I see things better when I'm high.
My work is not to judge, but classify.

Snapshot of My Sister and Brother-in-Law

The Fairbanks Pizza Hut—Jenny
And Bill are captured in the flash
Of his mom's camera. Bill smiles
Broadly and strokes his new mustache.

Jenny is staring off-right, glum
Over the baby's health; he's sick
So often, yet Bill says her talk
Of moving home is lunatic.

He's making more in one month's work
Than he could in six back in Austin.
She bites her lip and does her hair,
Eats out a lot. Her face grows wan.

The table's strewn with pizza crust,
Wadded napkins, pitchers of Coke.
The backdrop is a huge window:
The sun setting at three o'clock.

Sleeping with Shih Min Lu

Our beds were couches   During the day
But at night   We pulled them out
So that barely a foot   Separated ourselves

Grad students   In different fields
Lu's wife lived in Taiwan   With his parents
The woman I wouldn't marry And who wouldn't marry me
Was pregnant on the Big Island   Expecting soon

The house she'd inherited   Was in the path of a lava floe
Burn baby burn she'd say   When I telephoned

In the dark   I listened to symphonies
My headphones   Leaked the music
And Lu would cough   Clear his throat
Until I twirled the volume   To nearly nothing
Sometimes I'd wake   To hear his hand
Rustling under the sheets   I'd toss until he stopped

It was an understanding we had   Speech was impolite

One morning   Lu went crazy
Calling Taipei   Hanging up and calling again
He sobbed Chinese   Into the mouthpiece
The noises from his throat   Like air raid alarms

When I returned from class   A cousin was waiting
Mr. Lu is sick   Maybe he gone a while

For a week I slept   The lavish sleep of the unborn
Until the woman called   At six a.m.

Her house was on fire   It was a girl

Then Lu was back   He unpacked his overnight bag
Folded his shirts and pants   Neatly in their drawers

Night again   The overpowering perfume
Of honeycreepers   Night-blooming cereus
We pulled out our beds   And lay down quietly
Quietly   To breathe

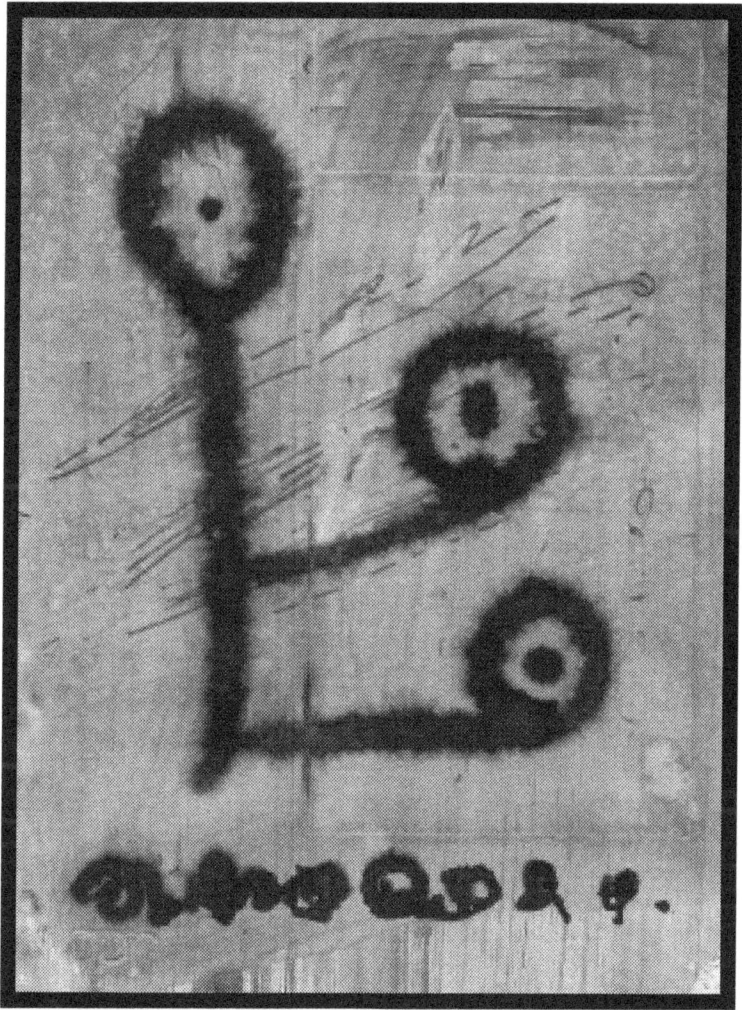

www.ingramcontent.com/pod-product-compliance
Lightning Source LLC
Chambersburg PA
CBHW031520040426
42445CB00009B/316